Penguin Books
Knots

Dr R. D. Laing was born in Glasgow and graduated from the
university there. He has worked as an army psychiatrist and with
various hospitals and clinics, including the Tavistock Institute
of Human Relations, where he did research into families from
1961 to 1967. His research is particularly concerned with
schizophrenia, families, and varieties of experience including
mind-expanding drugs.

His other books are *Self and Others*, *Sanity, Madness and the
Family* (with A. Esterson), *The Divided Self*, *The Politics
of Experience* and *The Bird of Paradise*, (all published by Penguins),
Reason and Violence (with David Cooper) and *Interpersonal
Perception* (with H. Phillipson and A. R. Lee).

D1255691

R. D. LAING · KNOTS

PENGUIN BOOKS

Penguin Books Ltd, Harmondsworth,
Middlesex, England
Penguin Books Australia Ltd, Ringwood,
Victoria, Australia
Penguin Books Canada Ltd,
41 Steelcase Road West,
Markham, Ontario, Canada

First published by Tavistock Publications 1970
Reprinted 1970, 1971
Published in Penguin Books for sale outside the
United Kingdom 1971
Published in Penguin Books for sale within the
United Kingdom 1972
Reprinted 1973, 1974
Copyright © The R. D. Laing Trust, 1970

Made and printed in Great Britain by
Hazell Watson & Viney Ltd, Aylesbury, Bucks
Set in Monotype Ehrhardt

The patterns delineated here have not yet been
classified by a Linnaeus of human bondage. They
are all, perhaps, strangely, familiar.
In these pages I have confined myself to laying out
only some of those I actually have seen. Words that
come to mind to name them are: knots, tangles,
fankles, *impasses*, disjunctions, whirligogs, binds.
I could have remained closer to the 'raw'
data in which these patterns appear. I could
have distilled them further towards an abstract
logico–mathematical calculus. I hope they are not so
schematized that one may not refer back to the
very specific experiences from which they derive;
yet that they are sufficiently independent of 'content', for
one to divine the final formal elegance in these
webs of *maya*.

April 1969   R.D.L.

I

They are playing a game. They are playing at not
playing a game. If I show them I see they are, I
shall break the rules and they will punish me.
I must play their game, of not seeing I see the game.

They are not having fun.
I can't have fun if they don't.
If I get them to have fun, then I can have fun with them.
Getting them to have fun, is not fun. It is hard work.
I might get fun out of finding out why they're not.
I'm not supposed to get fun out of working out why
they're not.
But there is even some fun in pretending to them I'm not
having fun finding out why they're not.

A little girl comes along and says: let's have fun.
But having fun is a waste of time, because it doesn't
help to figure out why they're *not* having fun.

How dare you have fun when Christ died on the Cross
for you! Was He having fun?

It is our duty to bring up our children to love,
honour and obey us.
If they don't, they must be punished,
otherwise we would not be doing our duty.

If they grow up to love, honour and obey us
we have been blessed for bringing them up properly.

If they grow up not to love, honour and obey us
     either we have brought them up properly
     or we have not:
if we have
     there must be something the matter with them;
if we have not
     there is something the matter with us.

A son should respect his father
He should not have to be taught to respect his father
It is something that is natural
That's how I've brought up my son anyway.

Of course a father must be worthy of respect
He can forfeit a son's respect
But I hope at least that my son will respect me, if
only for leaving him free to respect me or not.

There must be something the matter with him
  because he would not be acting as he does
    unless there was
  therefore he is acting as he is
  because there is something the matter with him

He does not think there is anything the matter with him
because
  one of the things that is
  the matter with him
  is that he does not think that there is anything
  the matter with him
therefore
  we have to help him realize that,
  the fact that he does not think there is anything
  the matter with him
  is one of the things that is
  the matter with him

there is something the matter with him
because he thinks
    there must be something the matter with us
for trying to help him to see
that there must be something the matter with him
to think that there is something the matter with us
for trying to help him to see that
    we are helping him
to see that
    we are not persecuting him
    by helping him
    to see we are not persecuting him
    by helping him
    to see that
    he is refusing to see
    that there is something the matter with
        him
    for not seeing there is something the matter
        with him

for not being grateful to us
for at least trying to help him
to see that there is something the matter with
him
for not seeing that there must be something the
matter with him
for not seeing that there must be something the
matter with him
for not seeing that there is something the matter
with him
for not seeing that there is something the matter
with him

for not being grateful

that we never tried to make him
feel grateful

It is the duty of children to respect their parents
And it is the duty of parents to teach their children
to respect them,
by setting them a good example.

Parents who do not set their children a good example
don't deserve respect.
If we do set them a good example
we believe they will grow up to be grateful to us
when they become parents themselves.

If he is cheeky
he doesn't respect you
for not punishing him
for not respecting you

You shouldn't spoil a child.
It's the easy way, to do what they want
but they won't respect you for letting them get away
with it when they grow up.

He won't respect you
    if you don't punish him
        for not respecting you.

My mother loves me.
    I feel good.
I feel good because she loves me.

I am good because I feel good
I feel good because I am good
My mother loves me because I am good.

My mother does not love me.
    I feel bad.
I feel bad because she does not love me
    I am bad because I feel bad
I feel bad because I am bad
I am bad because she does not love me
She does not love me because I am bad.

I don't feel good
therefore I am bad
therefore no one loves me.

I feel good
therefore I am good
therefore everyone loves me.

I am good
You do not love me
therefore you are bad. So I do not love you.

I am good
You love me
therefore you are good. So I love you.

I am bad
You love me
therefore you are bad.

Mother loves me
    because she is good
I am bad, to think she is bad
    therefore if I am good
        she is good
            and loves me
    because I am good
    to know she is good.

I am bad
    to doubt she punishes me for doubting
        she loves me by punishing me
    for doubting she loves me.

She says
    it must be *her* fault
    if I doubt she loves me.

She feels bad because
    I don't think she loves me because
        she feels bad when I don't think she loves me.

She feels
    it is her fault
    that I can be so cruel
    as to doubt she loves me
    when she makes me feel cruel,
    to think she tries to make me feel cruel.

To be kind is good. To be cruel is bad.

It is bad to feel mother is cruel to me, and hence bad.

Mother is cruel to me
but she is only being cruel to be kind
because I thought she was cruel when
she was cruel
in punishing me
because I was cruel to her
to think she was cruel to me
for punishing me
     for thinking she was cruel
for punishing me
     for thinking . . . . .

You are cruel
     to make me feel bad to think
          I am cruel to make you feel cruel
       by my feeling bad that you can be so cruel as to think
          I don't love you, when you know I do.

If you don't know I do there must be something the matter
with you.

it hurts Jack
to think
that Jill thinks he is hurting her
by (him) being hurt
to think
that she thinks he is hurting her
by making her feel guilty
at hurting him
by (her) thinking
that he is hurting her
by (his) being hurt
to think
that she thinks he is hurting her
by the fact that
                    da capo sine fine

2

Once upon a time, when Jack was little,
he wanted to be with his mummy all the time
and was frightened she would go away

later, when he was a little bigger,
he wanted to be away from his mummy
and was frightened that
she wanted him to be with her all the time

when he grew up he fell in love with Jill
and he wanted to be with her all the time
and was frightened she would go away

when he was a little older,
he did not want to be with Jill all the time
he was frightened
that she wanted to be with him all the time, and
that she was frightened
that he did not want to be with her all the time

Jack frightens Jill he will leave her
because he is frightened she will leave him.

Jack is afraid Jill is like his mother
Jill is afraid Jack is like her mother

Jack is afraid
        Jill thinks he is like her mother
and that   Jill is afraid
                Jack thinks she is like his mother

Jill is afraid
        Jack thinks she is like his mother
and that   Jack is afraid
                Jill thinks he is like her mother

Jack wants to devour his mother and be devoured by her
later, he oscillates between wanting to devour her but
not wanting to be devoured by her, and not wanting to
devour her but wanting her to devour him.

Later still, he does not want to devour her and does
not want her to devour him.

Jack feels Jill is devouring him.

He is devoured
    by his devouring fear of
    being devoured by
    her devouring desire
for *him* to devour *her*.

He feels she is eating him
by her demand to be eaten by him

Two people who originally
wished to devour and be devoured
are devouring and being devoured

She is devoured, by him being devoured by
        her devouring desire to be devoured
He is devoured by her being devoured
        by him not devouring her

He is being devoured
        by his dread of being devoured
She is being devoured
        by her desire to be devoured

His dread of being devoured
arises from his dread of being devoured by his devouring
Her desire to be devoured
arises from her dread of her desire to devour

I don't respect myself
I can't respect anyone who respects me.
I can only respect someone who does not respect me.

I respect Jack
because he does not respect me

I despise Tom
because he does not despise me

Only a despicable person
can respect someone as despicable as me

I cannot love someone I despise

Since I love Jack
I cannot believe he loves me

What proof can he give?

Jill feels safe to be angry with Jack
because Jack does nothing

She is angry with Jack
because he does nothing

She is angry with Jack
because he does not frighten her

He does not frighten her
because, doing nothing, he is useless.

She feels safe with him,
therefore she despises him

She clings to him
because he does not frighten her

She despises him
because she clings to him
because he does not frighten her

Jill knows she is inferior
therefore, she is superior to anyone who thinks she
is superior to him.

JILL   I am frightened
JACK   Don't be frightened
JILL   I am frightened to be frightened when you
       tell me I ought not to feel frightened

       frightened
       frightened to be frightened
       not frightened to be frightened

       not frightened
       frightened not to be frightened
       not frightened to be not frightened

JILL   I'm upset you are upset
JACK   I'm not upset
JILL   I'm upset that you're not upset that I'm
        upset you're upset
JACK   I'm upset that you're upset that I'm not
        upset that you're upset that I'm upset,
        when I'm not.

JILL   You put me in the wrong
JACK   I am not putting you in the wrong
JILL   You put me in the wrong for thinking you
        put me in the wrong.

JACK   Forgive me
JILL   No
JACK   I'll never forgive you for not forgiving me

JILL   You think I am stupid
JACK   I don't think you're stupid
JILL   I must be stupid to think you think I'm
        stupid if you don't: or you must be lying.
        I am stupid every way:
        to think I'm stupid, if I am stupid
        to think I'm stupid, if I'm not stupid
        to think you think I'm stupid, if you don't.

JILL   I'm ridiculous
JACK   No you are not
JILL   I'm ridiculous to feel ridiculous when I'm not.
        You must
            be laughing at me
       for feeling you are laughing at me
           if you are not laughing at me.

How clever has one to be to be stupid?
The others told her she was stupid. So she made
herself stupid in order not to see how stupid
they were to think she was stupid,
because it was bad to think they were stupid.
She preferred to be stupid and good,
rather than bad and clever.

It is bad to be stupid: she needs to be clever
to be so good and stupid.
It is bad to be clever, because this shows
how stupid they were
to tell her how stupid she was.

It is boring that you are frightened
you are boring me by being interested in me.

In trying to be interesting,
you are *very* boring.

You are frightened of being boring, you
try to be interesting by not being interested,
but are interested only in not being boring.

You are not interested in me.
You are only interested that I be interested in you.

You pretend to be bored
because I am not interested
        that you are frightened
                that I am not frightened
that you are not interested in me.

JACK   The trouble with you is that you are envious
        of me
JILL   The trouble with you is that's what you think

JACK   You never give me credit for anything.
        You can't bear to admit that I've got it.
JILL   That's where you go wrong. You can't bear
        to admit I don't care.

JACK   You're just like my mother,
JILL   You certainly treat me like her
JACK   Well don't behave like her then
JILL   You're trying to destroy me *because* you hate her.

JACK   Can't you stop projecting. You're the one
        that's frigid
JILL   I wasn't when I met you.

JACK   You might try not biting off your cunt to
        spite my prick
JILL   When you get to that level I feel hopeless
JACK   That's a start anyway. That's the first time
        today you've admitted any feeling of inadequacy.

JILL   Can't we just be friends
JACK   Of course. I'm friends with you all the time.

I'm happy you're happy
I'm unhappy you're unhappy

Jack's unhappy that Jill's unhappy
Jill's unhappy that Jack's unhappy
    that Jill's unhappy that Jack's unhappy
        that Jill's unhappy

Jill is guilty to be unhappy
    if Jack is unhappy that Jill is unhappy . . . . .

Jack is guilty that Jill is unhappy
    because he feels that he should make her happy

Jill feels guilty
    that Jack feels guilty
        that Jill feels guilty
            that Jack feels guilty

He can't be happy
	when there is so much suffering in the world
She can't be happy
	if he is unhappy

She wants to be happy
He does not feel entitled to be happy

She wants him to be happy
and he wants her to be happy

He feels guilty if he is happy
and guilty if she is not happy

She wants both to be happy

He wants her to be happy

So they are both unhappy

He accuses her of being selfish
	because she is trying to get him to be happy
	so that she can be happy

She accuses him of being selfish
	because he is only thinking of himself

He thinks he is thinking of the whole cosmos

She thinks she is mainly thinking of him
because she loves him

How can she be happy
when the man she loves is unhappy

He feels she is blackmailing him
by making him feel guilty
because she is unhappy that he is unhappy

She feels he is trying to destroy her love for him
by accusing her of being selfish
when the trouble is
that she can't be so selfish as to be happy
when the man she loves is unhappy

She feels that there must be something wrong with her
to love someone who can be so cruel
as to destroy her love for him
and is too guilty to be happy, and is unhappy because
he is guilty

He feels that he is unhappy because he is guilty
to be happy when others are unhappy and that he made
a mistake to marry someone who can only think of
happiness.

She has started to drink
    as a way to cope
    that makes her less able to cope

the more she drinks
the more frightened she is of becoming a drunkard

the more drunk
the less frightened of being drunk

the more frightened of being drunk when not drunk
    the more not frightened drunk
    the more frightened not drunk

the more she destroys herself
the more frightened of being destroyed by him

the more frightened of destroying him
the more she destroys herself

JACK   You are a pain in the neck
To stop *you* giving me a pain in the neck
I protect my neck by tightening my neck muscles,
which gives me the pain in the neck
      you are.

JILL   My head aches through trying to stop you
giving me a headache.

Narcissus fell in love with his image, taking it to
be another.

Jack falls in love with Jill's image of Jack, taking
it to be himself.
She must not die, because then he would lose himself.
He is jealous in case any one else's image is reflected
in her mirror.

Jill is a distorting mirror to herself.
Jill has to distort herself to appear undistorted
to herself.

To undistort herself, she finds Jack to distort her
distorted image in his distorting mirror
She hopes that his distortion of her distortion may
undistort her image without her having to distort herself.

I never got what I wanted.
I always got what I did not want.
What I want
       I shall not get.

Therefore, to get it
       I must not want it
since I get only what I don't want.

       what I want, I can't get
       what I get, I don't want

   I can't get it
because I want it
   I get it
because I don't want it.

I want what I can't get
because
       what I can't get *is* what I want

I don't want what I can get
because
       what I can get *is* what I don't want

I never get what I want
I never want what I get

I get what I deserve
I deserve what I get.

I have it,
    therefore I deserve it

I deserve it
    because I have it.

You have not got it
    therefore you do not deserve it

You do not deserve it
    because you have not got it

You have not got it
    because you do not deserve it

You do not deserve it
therefore you have not got it.

I am not entitled to what I have
therefore everything I have is stolen.
If I've got it,
and I am not entitled to it,
I *must* have stolen it,
because I am not entitled to it.

I am not entitled to it
because I have stolen it.

I have stolen it
therefore I am not entitled to it.

I am not entitled to it
therefore I must have stolen it.

Or, it has been given to me as a special favour
by someone who is entitled to it
so I am expected to be grateful for all I have
because what I have
has been *given*, not stolen.

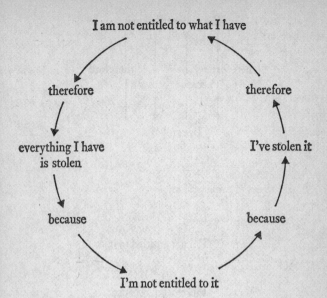

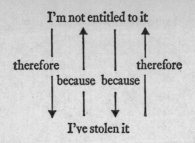

I'm not entitled to it

therefore   because   because   therefore

I've stolen it

I'm not entitled to it

therefore | because

I've stolen it

Positive and negative binds.

Negative: Can't win. Everything I do is wrong.
Positive: Can't lose. Everything I do is right.

I do it, because it is right.
It is right, because I do it.

I want it
I get it
therefore I am good

I want it
I don't get it
therefore I am bad

I am bad
      because I didn't get it

I am bad
      because I wanted what I didn't get

I must take care
      to get what I want
      and want what I get
   and not get what I don't want

| good | get | want | can |
| bad | not–get | not–want | cannot |

I can get what I want
I can't get what I want
I can get what I don't want
I can't get what I don't want

I tend to not get what I want
So
      to get what I want
      I pretend not to want it

I am bad to want what I can't get
I haven't got it
      therefore I am bad to want it

If I am bad to want it
I shall be no less bad for getting it

I am bad to feel bad, and
      bad to feel good
because the badder one is
      the less bad one feels

There is something the matter with me because I do
not feel anything the matter with me

What one has,
     has been given one
therefore everything one has
     one is entitled to.
The more one has
     the better one is
          because the more one has been rewarded
               for being good.
Therefore I get better and better
     through 'making' more and more

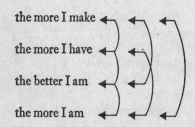

All I have has been given me and is mine

If I have it, I must have been given it
Therefore it is mine.

I haven't it
but I can get it
therefore,
        because I have been given the capacity to get it
it is mine.

It is not mine
but it has been given me and I have it
therefore I am grateful for what I have, or
        have been given.

But I resent being grateful
because if I have been given it, it has not always been mine.
therefore, if I don't feel grateful
        I won't have been given it
therefore, it is (past, present, future) eternally mine.

$$\left[\begin{matrix} \text{If it is mine} \\ \qquad \text{it is not me} \end{matrix} \right. \qquad \qquad \text{Moderato}$$

<pre>
⎡ If it is mine   Moderato
⎣   it is not me 1

⎡ If it is not mine
⎣   it is not me 2

  If it is not me   ⎤
          it is not mine   ⎦ 3

  If it is me   ⎤
          it is mine   ⎦ 4

But,
        if it is mine
                  it is not me 1
    and if it is not me
                  it is not mine 3

Therefore,
        if,
        if it is not me
                  it is not mine 3

    and *if,*
        if it is not mine
                  it is not me 2

    and *if,*
        if mine
                  it is not me 1

    then,
        if it's not me
                  it's mine 5
</pre>

42

If it's not me it's mine 5
If it's mine it's not me 1

If it's mine it's not me 1

If it's not me
        It's not mine 3
if it's not mine
        it's not me 2
if it's not me
        it's mine 5

If,   if it's mine
        it is not me 1
  if it is not me
        it's not mine 3

then,
If it's mine, it's not mine 6

If,   if it's mine, it's not mine 6
  ·if(1234/13/3215/51132513)

poco a poco accelerando al fine

    then,
      if it's not mine,
        it is not me 2
      and if it's not me
        it's mine 5
      if it's mine
        it's not me, ...1
    if,   if it's not me
        it's not mine 3
      if it's not me
        it's mine 5

    then,
      If it's mine
        it's me 7

if,   if it's mine

        it's me 7

   if (1234133215511325136625135)

   if it's me, it's mine 4

   if it's mine it's not me 1

then if it's not me it's not mine   ...\...3

hence,

   If it's not mine it's me 8

   If it's not mine it's me 8

        if (1.....577413)

   if it's me

        it's mine 4

   if it's mine it's not mine 6

   if it's not mine it's not me 2

   if it's not me

        it's mine 5

Then,

   If it's not mine it's mine 9

   If it's not mine it's mine 9

        if (1.....3884625)

   if it's mine it's not mine 6

        if it's not mine

             it's not me 2

   if it's not me it's mine 5

   if it's mine it's me 7

Then,   if it's me it's not me   ....10 (cf. an

   if it's not me it's mine 5   enharmonic

   if it's mine   change)

        it's me 7

   If it's me it's not mine 11

   If it's not mine

        it's not me 2

   if it's not me

        it's mine

44

if it's mine it's not mine
if it's not mine it's mine
    if it's mine is not me
    if not me is not mine
    if not mine
              is me
    if me is not mine
    if not mine is not me
then, if not me, it is me
if not me, it is me
if it is me, it is not mine
if it is not mine it is not me
if it is not me, it is me
if it is me
    it is not mine
if it is not mine
    it is me
if it is me, it is mine
    if it is mine
              it is not me
therefore if it is not me
              it is mine
      if it is mine it is mine

if it is mine it is mine
if it is mine it is not mine
if it is not mine it is mine
if it is mine, it is mine
if it is mine, it is not mine
if it is not mine,
                    it is me
if it is me it is mine
if it is mine it is not me
if it is not me it is me
if it is me

            it is not me
            if it is not me
            it is me
if it's me, if it's not me
if it's not me, if it's me
if it's me if it's me
if it's me if it's not me
if it's not me if it's not me
it's me if it's not me
if it's not me, it's me
if it's me it's not me
if it's not me it's me
if it's me,
if it's not me.
if it's me

if it's not me
if it's me
if it's not me
if it's me
if it's not me, it's me
if it's not me it's not me
it's not me if it's me
if it's me it's me
it's me if it's not me
if it's not me, it's not me
if it's not me, it's me
it's me if it's me
if it's not me it's not me
it's not me if it's not me
if it's me, it's me
if it's me, it's me
I am it
if it is not me
if it is not me, I am it, if I am not it, I
am it, if I am it, I am not it

She wants him to want her
He wants her to want him

To get him to want her
     she pretends she wants him

To get her to want him
     he pretends he wants her

Jack wants	Jill wants
Jill's want of Jack	Jack's want of Jill
so	so
Jack tells Jill	Jill tells Jack
Jack wants Jill	Jill wants Jack

a perfect contract

Jill and Jack both want to be wanted.

Jill wants Jack because he wants to be wanted
Jack wants Jill because she wants to be wanted.

Jill wants Jack to want
    *Jill to want
        Jack's want of her want
            for his want of her want of

Jack's want that Jill wants
    Jack to want
        Jill to want
            Jack's want of her want
                for his want of
                    her to want Jack to want*

                        *repeat *sine fine*

She does not get what she wants from him
    so she feels that he is mean
She cannot give him what he wants from her
    so she feels that he is greedy

    He does not get what he wants from her
        so he feels that she is mean
and
    he cannot give her what she wants from him
        so he feels that she is greedy

Jill thinks Jack is mean and greedy
Jack thinks Jill is mean and greedy
the more Jill feels that Jack is mean
the more greedy Jack feels Jill to be
the more Jill feels Jack is greedy
the more mean Jack feels Jill to be
the more greedy Jack feels Jill to be
        the more mean Jill feels Jack to be
        the more mean Jill feels Jack to be
the more greedy Jack feels Jill to be
Jack feels Jill is greedy
            because Jill feels Jack is mean
Jill feels Jack is mean
    because Jack feels Jill is greedy
Jack feels Jill is mean
            because Jill feels Jack is greedy
Jill feels Jack is greedy
    because Jack feels Jill is mean

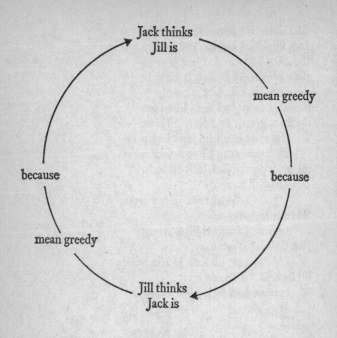

The more
    Jack feels Jill is mean to feel he is greedy
the more
    Jill feels Jack is mean
        to feel she is mean to feel he is greedy
           to feel she is mean

The more Jill feels Jack is mean
    to feel she is mean to feel he is greedy to feel she is mean
the more Jack feels Jill is mean
    to feel
        Jack is mean
           to feel she is mean
           to feel he is greedy
           to feel she is mean
    because she does not give him what he wants

He wants her to be more generous
    in her judgement about him,
namely, not feel he is mean
    to feel she is mean
        to feel he is greedy
           to feel she is mean
    to feel he is mean
        to feel she is mean
        to feel he is greedy
        to feel she is mean

She feels
    he is asking too much (greedy)
    to expect *her*,
    not to feel he is asking too much (greedy)
    to expect her
    not to feel he is mean and greedy
        to feel she is mean
        to feel he is greedy
            to feel *she* is mean
    to feel he is mean
    to feel she is mean
    to feel he is greedy
    to feel she is greedy
when all *she* wants is that
    he be more generous in his judgement about her

namely, not to feel she is mean
        to feel he is mean
        to feel she is greedy
        to feel he is mean
    to feel she is mean
        to feel he is mean
        to feel she is greedy
        to feel he is mean
to want her to be more generous in her judgement about him
namely,

3

If I don't know I don't know
                    I think I know
If I don't know I know
                    I think I don't know

There is something I don't know
		that I am supposed to know.
I don't know *what* it is I don't know,
		and yet am supposed to know,
and I feel I look stupid
		if I seem both not to know it
				and not know *what* it is I don't know.
Therefore I pretend I know it.
		This is nerve-racking
		since I don't know what I must pretend to know.
Therefore I pretend to know everything.

I feel you know what I am supposed to know
but you can't tell me what it is
because you don't know that I don't know what it is.

You may know what I don't know, but not
				that I don't know it,
and I can't tell you. So you will have to tell me everything.

Jack can see that he sees
            what Jill can't see
     and that Jill can't see Jill can't see it

Jack can see that he sees
      what Jill can't see
but Jack can't see
      that Jill can't see
            that Jill can't see it

Jack tries to get Jill to see
      that Jack can see
      what Jill can't see
but Jack can't see
      that Jill can't see that Jill can't see it

Jack sees
            there is something Jill can't see
and Jack sees
            that Jill can't see she can't see it

Although Jack can see Jill can't see she can't see it
he can't see that *he* can't see it himself

Jack can see
1.   there is something Jill can't see
2.   and that she can see there is something she can't see
3.   but that she can't see *what* she can't see
        although
(Jack can see that)
4.   she can see Jack can see whatever it is
                she can see she can't see
                but can't see what.

Jack thinks
            he does not know
        what he thinks
            Jill thinks
            he does not know

But Jill thinks Jack does know it.

So Jill does not know
            she does not know
        that Jack does not know
        that Jill thinks
        that Jack does know
and Jack does not know he does not know
        that Jill does not know she does not know
        that Jack does not know
            that Jill thinks Jack knows
what Jack thinks he does not know

Jack doesn't know he knows
and he doesn't know
    Jill does not know.

Jill doesn't know she doesn't know,
    and doesn't know
        that Jack doesn't know he knows
    and that he does not know Jill does not know.
They have no problem.

Jack thinks that
      what he knows that Jill does not,
is that there is nothing to be known
of the order Jill is seeking to know,
but that Jill has to discover this for herself.

Jill thinks
      Jack knows what
      Jill thinks Jill doesn't know.
Jack does not know
      there is something to know
      that Jill thinks
            she does not and
            Jack does.
So Jack persuades Jill that there is nothing to know.

Jack
       knows he does not know
and sees that Jill
               does not know she knows.
By telling Jack
       what Jack knows he does not know
Jill helps Jack to help Jill
       to know she knows
       what she does not know she knows.

Jill however
       thinks
               she knows she does not know
and that Jack knows
       she knows she does not know
and that Jack knows
       what Jill does not know.

Jill thinks
   that there is something she knows
   and that she does not know she knows it.
  She thinks Jack does not know it
   and that Jack knows he does not.
Jill hopes that through Jack
  Jill will
  know that she knows
  what Jack knows he does not –
but only if Jack can realize
  that Jill knows
  what Jack knows Jack does not
  and Jill does not know she does.

Jack knows he does not know
Jill thinks she knows what Jack does not know, but
she does not know he does not know it.
Jack does not know
  Jill does not know he does not know,
and thinks she knows what he knows he doesn't.

Jack believes Jill.
Jack now does not know he does not know.
One happy ending.

Jack thinks Jack sees what he does not,*
and that Jill sees what she does not see.

Jill believes Jack.
She now thinks she sees what Jack thinks Jack sees
  and that Jack sees it too.
They may now both be completely wrong.

* This is ambiguous. Jack thinks he is seeing an illusion;
 is he right or wrong? Jack thinks he is not under an illusion.
 Is he right or wrong? Try it anyway.

Jack does not see something.
Jill thinks Jack does see it.
Jack thinks Jack does see it and Jill does not.
Jill does not see herself what
    she thinks Jack does see.

Jack tells Jill
        what Jack thinks Jill does not see.
Jill realizes
    that,
        if Jack thinks
            Jill does not see *that*,
            which Jill thinks she does,
        Jack does not see
            what Jill thought
                Jack saw.

Jill thinks
        Jack thinks
            Jill does not see something.

Jack does think
        Jill sees it
but Jack does not see
        Jill thinks
        Jack thinks
        Jill does not see.

Jill thinks she can't see what she thinks Jack can see,
and that Jack himself thinks that
    Jill does not see it.

Jack sees Jill *does* see it
    that she thinks she does not,
and that she thinks
    he thinks
        she does not

But Jack can't see what Jill can't see
    whereby she thinks she can't see what Jack thinks she
                                   can,
      and thinks he thinks she can't.

For example:

Jill thinks
    Jack thinks Jill is stupid.
Jack does not think Jill is stupid,
but cannot see why
    Jill thinks Jack thinks Jill is,
when Jack does not.
Nor can Jill, except that Jack is lying.

Jack sees
    Jill can't see Jill can't see
and that
    Jill can't see
        Jack can see and
           see he sees
    what Jill can't see she can't.
Jack tries to get Jill to
    realize that there may be something
    she can't see she can't see.

Jill thinks Jill sees it
    and can see that Jack thinks
        Jill thinks she sees it
    but that Jack thinks
        Jill can't see she can't.
Jill thinks
    Jack can't see he can't see
        what he thinks he can,
    and that he can't see (therefore)
        that she sees what he thinks he sees
           but doesn't.

Jack thinks he knows
Jill thinks Jill does not know
Jack tells Jill
    what Jack knows
    and knows he knows
    and knows Jill does not know
    and knows Jill sometimes
        thinks she knows
            when she does not.

Sometimes Jack feels
Jill idealizes Jack, making him
omniscient (omnipotent)
so he points out to Jill
that he is only human,
he does not know everything and can't do everything.

Jack says Jill
makes Jack
omnipotent, to remain impotent, to make Jack
impotent to make her potent, to
destroy Jack's
potency, which she envies . . . . .

Jill thinks Jack is wrong.

Jack thinks
      he does not know what (he can see)
            Jill thinks Jack knows,
    and that Jill knows
            what Jill thinks Jack knows,
                that he thinks
                      he does not.

Jack tells Jill:
      'You think I know this,
           but I don't.'
Jill thinks he does, but refuses to tell her.

Jack knows he does not know,
but he does not know that Jill does not know
    she does not know he knows he does not know.

Jack thinks that
    Jack ⌈ knows Jack does not know

            knows Jill does know

            knows Jill does not know she knows

            knows Jill thinks Jack knows

            knows Jill thinks

                Jack does not know Jack knows
      ⌊

and that Jill realizes that that is what he thinks,
but that she thinks he is wrong.

Jack sees that
      Jill does not know
      Jack does not know what
      Jill thinks
      Jack knows.
But Jack can't see
      why Jill does not know
      that Jack does not know
      what Jill thinks
      he knows.

Jack realizes that he knows
    Jill does not know
        Jack knows
        he doesn't know
  what she thinks
        he does
but that this is not what she thinks he knows.

Moreover Jack sees that Jill herself knows what Jill
thinks Jack knows, but that Jill does not realize
she knows it.

Jack sees that
    Jill knows
        what Jill thinks
            Jack knows
and that Jill does not know
        she knows
        and Jack knows he does not.
He cannot tell Jill
        what it is
since, although he can see Jill knows it,
he does not know it himself.

Jill does not know
     Jack does not know X,
and Jack cannot tell her more than that there is
something, he does not know what,
     he does not know.

There is something Jack can't see.
He knows there is something he can't see,
but doesn't know what it is that he can't see.
But Jack can see Jill can see
     that Jack can't see something.

Jack doesn't know
     what he doesn't know
but he thinks
     Jill knows whatever the something is which he doesn't
                                      know.

Jack can't tell Jill what he
        wants Jill to tell him.
Jill can't tell him either
because although Jill knows X
Jill does not know
        that Jack does not know X.

Jack can see
that Jill knows
he realizes that she
does not know she knows X.
Jill can only discover
she knows it
by realizing what Jack does not

But Jill
cannot see what
        Jack does not know.
If she did she would be glad to tell him.

Jack can see he sees
      what he can see Jill can't see
and he can see
      that Jill can't see that she can't see
but he can't see WHY
      Jill can't see that Jill can't see.

Jill
      can see that he does not understand her
and can see that he can't see that he doesn't:
and she can see
      that he can't see that he can't see
            she sees he can't see he doesn't.
Why does she still feel confused?
She cannot understand why he can't see that
she sees that he can't see that he does not understand.

Jill can see Jack can't see,
        and can't see he can't see.
Jill can see WHY
    Jack can't see,
but Jill cannot see WHY
    Jack can't see he can't see.

Jack 'sees' Jill is blind
        and that Jill can't see she is.
Jack realizes they both are.
If the blind must lead the blind, it is as well
that the leader knows he is.

Jack can't see he can't see
and can't see
    Jill can't see Jill can't see it.
and vice versa

4

Jack is afraid of Jill
Jill is afraid of Jack

Jack is more afraid of Jill   Jill is more afraid of Jack
    if Jack thinks   if Jill thinks
       that Jill thinks   that Jack thinks
that Jack is afraid of Jill   that Jill is afraid of Jack

Since Jack is afraid
       that Jill will think that
            Jack is afraid
       Jack pretends that
            Jack is not afraid of Jill
so that Jill will be more afraid of Jack

and since Jill is afraid
       that Jack will think that
            Jill is afraid
       Jill pretends that
            Jill is not afraid of Jack

Thus
       Jack tries to make Jill afraid
            by not being afraid of Jill
       and Jill tries to make Jack afraid
            by not being afraid of Jack

The more Jack is afraid of Jill
    the more frightened is Jack that
        Jill will think
            that Jack is afraid

the more Jill is afraid of Jack
    the more frightened is Jill that
        Jack will think
            that Jill is afraid

the more afraid Jack is of Jill
    the more frightened Jack is
not to be frightened of Jill
because it is very dangerous not to be afraid when
faced with one so dangerous

Jack is frightened because Jill is dangerous
Jill appears dangerous because Jack is frightened

the more afraid Jill is of Jack
    the more frightened Jill is
not to be frightened of Jack

The more Jack is frightened not to be frightened
the more frightened he is to appear frightened

the more frightened Jill is
                not to be frightened
the more frightened Jill is
        to appear to be frightened

the more frightened each is,
                the less frightened each appears to be

Jack is frightened
        not to be frightened at Jill
and to appear to be frightened at Jill
and that Jill be not frightened at Jack

                Jill is frightened
                not to be frightened at Jack
        and to appear to be frightened at Jack
and that Jack be not frightened at Jill

Jack therefore tries to frighten Jill
by appearing not to be frightened
        that she appears not to be frightened

and Jill tries to frighten Jack
        by appearing not to be frightened
                that he appears not to be frightened

The more Jack tries to appear not to be frightened
    the more frightened he is that
        he is not frightened
    that he appears to be frightened
    that Jill is not frightened

the more Jill tries to appear not to be frightened
    the more frightened she is that
        she is not frightened
    that she appears to be frightened
    that Jack is not frightened

The more this is so
    the more Jack frightens Jill
    by appearing not to be frightened
and the more Jill frightens Jack
    by appearing not to be frightened

Can each become frightened of being
    frightened and of frightening
instead of being frightened
    not to be frightened
    and not to frighten?

Can Jack and Jill
      terrified that each and the other are not terrified
become
      terrified that each and other are terrified, and
eventually,
      not terrified that each and other not be terrified?

5

All in all
Each man in all men
all men in each man

All being in each being
Each being in all being

All in each
Each in all

All distinctions are mind, by mind, in mind, of mind
No distinctions no mind to distinguish

One is inside
then outside what one has been inside
One feels empty
because there is nothing inside oneself
One tries to get inside oneself
    that inside of the outside
    that one was once inside
    once one tries to get oneself inside what
    one is outside:
    to eat and to be eaten
to have the outside inside and to be
    inside the outside

But this is not enough. One is trying to get
the inside of what one is outside inside, and to
get inside the outside. But one does not get
inside the outside by getting the outside inside
for;
although one is full inside of the inside of the outside
one is on the outside of one's own inside
and by getting inside the outside
one remains empty because
while one is on the inside
even the inside of the outside is outside
and inside oneself there is still nothing
There has never been anything else
and there never will be

I am doing it
the it I am doing is
the I that is doing it
the I that is doing it is
the it I am doing
it is doing the I that am doing it
I am being done by the it I am doing
it is doing it

One is afraid of
the self that is afraid of
the self that is afraid of
the self that is afraid
One may perhaps speak of reflections

Although innumerable beings have been led to Nirvana
no being has been led to Nirvana

Before one goes through the gate
one may not be aware there is a gate
One may think there is a gate to go through
and look a long time for it
without finding it
One may find it and
it may not open
If it opens one may be through it
As one goes through it
one sees that the gate one went through
was the self that went through it
no one went through a gate
there was no gate to go through
no one ever found a gate
no one ever realized there was never a gate

By those who know the discourse on dharmas
as like unto a raft
dharmas should be forsaken, still more so
no–dharmas

Hearing that dharmas, and still more so, no–dharmas
should be forsaken
some are of the opinion that there is no gate
that is their opinion
there is no way of knowing except to go
through it

a finger points to the moon

Put the expression
    a finger points to the moon, in brackets
    (a finger points to the moon)
The statement:
    'A finger points to the moon is in brackets'
is an attempt to say that all that is in the bracket
    (   )
is, as to that which is not in the bracket,
what a finger is to the moon

Put all possible expressions in brackets
Put all possible forms in brackets
and put the brackets in brackets

Every expression, and every form,
is to what is expressionless and formless
what a finger is to the moon
all expressions and all forms
point to the expressionless and formless

the proposition
    'All forms point to the formless'
is itself a formal proposition

Not,
    as finger to moon
    so form to formless
but,
    as finger is to moon
    so

        ⌐ all possible expressions, forms, propositions, ¬
          including this one, made or yet to be made,
        L together with the brackets

    are to

What an interesting finger
    let me suck it

It's not an interesting finger
    take it away

The statement is pointless
The finger is speechless